SINSATIONS

REGGIE JOHNSON

SINSATIONS

Copyright © 2018 Reggie Johnson/Rad Press Publishing

Cover Design by: Mitch Green

All rights reserved. No part of this publication may be reproduced, distributed or conveyed without the permission of the publisher.

First printing 2018

REGGIE JOHNSON

PRELUDE

We all fall victim
Switching between being the predator and the prey
From one's life choices
In this Darwinistic world
How much greed are you willing to partake in to get further?
How lazy can you become so you can just get by in life?
How jealous will you become at the hand of another person's success?
How much are you willing to lose in order to succumb to one's desires?
And when you consume everything in your surroundings...
Answer this one question...
Are you proud of yourself after all you did?
Roll the dice...
Hopefully luck's on your side when you fall into sin

SINSATIONS

LUST

REGGIE JOHNSON

Insatiable thoughts that cloud the mind eventually creating a thunderstorm of events ranging from sexual to intellectual stimulation

CARNAL

Carnal
Almost feral in the way...
We become animals basking over the flesh
Love is a carcass that we continue to feed on
And to feed on and feed on...
Until the same redness of the remains
Becomes a drug that our bodies cannot get enough of
Fucking carnivores we are
That's what love makes us do

REGGIE JOHNSON

IVORY LIZARDS
FEATURING MITCH GREEN

the tapestries are half done on the walls above the open kitchen. there are potholes spotting the floor at where the worn wooden table sits and the bare heels of a woman in a bathrobe stands. we slowly pan up, framing pasty legs sleeved in tape and clay. her lips are wrist wiped, smeared boisterous up her left cheek and down across her cold purple breasts.

towering above the threshold of her crown, we see an unshaven phallus half erect, sprung between her legs. eyelashes flash blue irises to spear brightly among mediocre makeup and fibers of false hair falling out. there are polished toes, chipped red and another naked body on the couch in the next room.

this one is frail, wrangled to the soles of the vintage furniture, grain gouged to expose poor complexion and a broken fever, there blooms a garden, green and yellow from tongue; wallowed in wiry roots. contagious sensitivity is all that exists. the third alive, hangs from ceiling fans on fire with smoke detectors for eyes, the box television on the night stand speaks noise to ivory lizards

-Mitch Green

here stands a girl. unhappy with herself. her behavior. she reaches into her makeup bag and grabs her mahogany Maybelline to fix the lipstick that has been left on their cheeks, their t-shirts, their chests and you can figure out the rest.

she pulls her skirt up and fixes her hair. she picks up her shoes and carries them out to not awake the lizards from their slumber. and as she tip-toes through the living room, she sees all the excursions she just partook in and looks in disgust.

one guy, it was his first time. another, he was just out for his regular Saturday night cheating session. another, you could see dried tears on his face from crying in regret for the actions he just done. and all she could do is give a smirk for the part she played in all of this.

-*Reggie Johnson*

SINSATIONS

RELEASE

There were days I wanted to...
Just break abstinence and release
And your body too...
My mind would go that far
Then, you whisper something in my ear
And I go to mush
Just want to take you by the waist...
Take you to my place...
Have our lips meet when we're face to face and...

LA REINA DE LA ISLA
FEATURING HALFOFYOU

La reina de la isla
Su piel como el café y su sangre caliente
Como el suelo en que camina.
Sus besos de miel y sus abrazos de
Azúcar, quiero morir soñando en las miradas de sus ojos
Como vuela la reina, un ángel por el cielo y la dueña de la isla
Como canta la reina, llena de música y de ritmo de la isla, cada ciudadano su familia
Desde Santo Domingo se entrego a sus raíces
Pero ella carga la lengua de todos los paises
Como mueve, como baila, me entrego a sus sonrisas
Bienvenidos a la isla

-HalfOfYou

Isla del tesoro...
Cuando seguí el mapa, mi corazón se dirigió directamente a x, marca tu lugar
Que trotamos para llegar a las O que conducen a los abrazos y besos
Solo de lo que he imaginado durante tanto tiempo
Y lo anhelaba
El amor se mezcla con la lujuria
La actividad sexual se convierte en nuestra confianza
Las numerosas posibilidades de lo que estas manos pueden hacer
Estoy aquí para ser el guardián de los problemas que te preocupan
Deje que la oscuridad se ilumine con la luz de la luna, ya que brilla sobre la arena
Esta tierra es tu tierra
Y estoy aquí para compartirlo contigo
Por ti es donde estoy parado

-Reggie Johnson

SINSATIONS

MY HEROINE

It was a game we played
An addiction...
We became drug dependent off each other's love
To the point where the scratching became not of ourselves
But of walls as it reminds us the times we had together
Those...were the fun nights
And now, I'm going through withdrawals
Everything...reminds me of you
You became a passionfruit that I wanted to taste over and over
Like I bit an apple from the Garden of Eden
It was our sanctuary
And I miss how you blessed me each and every time

REGGIE JOHNSON

HOMELY LOWS
FEATURING MITCH GREEN

Foul jargon scrapples the wet disheveled walls made of decrepit foliage. Found outward turned ocean green are these handsome carbon imprints. As real as avalanches hailing downwind, apparitions in my skin. The takeover of ethereal post life charming air.

It is the homely lows that quake nervous.

-Mitch Green

Nails running down my spine ignite sparks that go off like dynamite creating firework after firework. It comes in fours like the day in July and I love how she does it independently. And add four more to treat me like you do on my birthday since we are already in our suits. You have the gifts that keep on giving.

It is the homely lows that make our highs that much more satisfying.

-Reggie Johnson

MUSH

This is what you did to me...

This feeling...

My bones become cotton candy

As the rest becomes things that you like

And you're buying everything that I'm selling

It's rare to find someone like you

Once found, I don't want to lose it

This feeling

Never...

Ever...

Just. Please. Stay.

REGGIE JOHNSON

PRETENDERS
FEATURING MITCH GREEN

It is on the breath of undressed
idols in undressed rooms.
The foreign lights and beauty
marks on pale lions.
The inaudible Beelzebub and the
white horse in wax.

Exhume us heavily.
Exhume us wholly.
Smoke us out.

Hands over the heat of invasion
Our bodies were temples to edge
death. Bad blood in bad men.
Pretenders at best.

-Mitch Green

Sweat glistens from your pores
As I lay relaxed in your shores
Our bodies dissolve into the bed
like the sand

Rest and relaxation at its best
Wanting to scream, "Life's a beach"

Let us play until the sun goes
down
Let us tire ourselves until we don't
have anymore energy

You cannot take this joy from us
This pure bliss
The mountainous heights we
reach when we peak
Pretenders at best until it all falls
down

-Reggie Johnson

GLUTTONY

REGGIE JOHNSON

Mass consumption to the point that it takes over your mental, emotional and physical state of being

SINSATIONS

INSATIABLE

My heart became your delicacy
Seasoned by jealousy
You did all you could when you wanted to mess with me
And when we were together, you wanted to be forever
Before we even got a chance to be
And when we're apart, you would blame all the problems on me
Venga, venga y solucionemos esto
Termina esta peleá con abrazos y besos

REGGIE JOHNSON

THE HAPPENING
FEATURING ASHLEY R. LUCAS

You want the whole world between your fingers and that frightens me. There's a certain look in your eyes, like you'd do absolutely anything to get it. Whatever it takes. Whatever it wants. Even me. Even you.

-*Ashley R. Lucas*

Eating...
It's eating away at my sanity
How one's comfort is found in discomfort
I'm tired of feeding off of it
Sick to my stomach
I just want to feel at ease again

-*Reggie Johnson*

INFORMATION OVERLOAD

We all are guilty of it
The mass of different media platforms
That are here for us to emulate, praise and hope
To one day be better than
Constant flow of information highways
Driving our every thought, action, choice, consequence
Like a car accident waiting to happen
If only, we can be unplugged for awhile

ZOMBIE
FEATURING ASHLEY R. LUCAS

When was the last time you valued something deemed valuable? When was the last time you chased after something that wasn't green or covered in flesh? I can tell that the pockets of your jeans are heavier than your heart. That the place you sleep is a trove of treasures and the place you dream is hollow as air. Are you okay with that? Being the prettiest and the biggest egg in the nest, but the only one with no life inside.

-Ashley R. Lucas

I don't know the last time I bought something valuable. The things I chased after that I thought was valuable ended up disintegrating into thin air just like my interests. I became numb by the consumption. For the masses. Validation granted, validation passes. Validation earned, validation lost. Validation gained, validation costs. Caught up in the thought I don't think we can even function normally. Like the bare minimum of being friends became so toxic, cannot even pretend. Cannot even depend on waiting for you to change. Waiting, waiting till you become a couch potato engulfed in your woes like I have become. Eating at them like they're Twinkies and donuts. All I have to say is that I should get my fat ass up and work it out once for all or continue to let it weigh on the both of us.

-Reggie Johnson

SINSATIONS

THE HUNGER
FEATURING ASHLEY R. LUCAS

You eat this love of mine like it's already fleeting. As if you're afraid that you'll look away for a moment and the plate will be torn from you. Wiped clean. Given to another to enjoy. You're loving me like you can't get enough, but it's too rash. Too much. Too fast.

-Ashley R. Lucas

I become numb. As the lovey-dovey coos became less rhythmic and more blues. Got caught up in seeing things black and white. And less colorful with the hues. I was colorful with my words didn't mean to peruse. You were hungry for love that you didn't take the time to digest the situation and the effects of your actions. And the reactions that would result. This one's on you, even though we both played a part.

-Reggie Johnson

REGGIE JOHNSON

UTILITY

Took my gullibility like a pawn
In your chess game
A speedy one, as if you have had your moves planned all along
Every nice gesture, every moment, every instance
As if, I was just a means to an end
A utility...
And I acted as a filler for the void in your life
Realizing you are nothing more of a damn leech
A leech in my life sucking everything for me just to die off in the end
I'm learning not to be that way
And it's thanks to you

SINSATIONS

GREED

REGGIE JOHNSON

The irresistible desire of something for personal gain

INFATUATION

The infatuation became contagious
Acceptance...
Validation...
It's like a medicine drip that permeates my psyche
Do you really like me for who I am?
And why do I care?
Not everyone is going to like you
And there's nothing we can do about it

ALL FOR LOVE

Consumption

More of myself falling to prey to a zombie drawn to love

Love that is housed in me

The only thing you've become is a Resident Evil

As you walk dead

A bite of me and now you turn me into something else

Someone else

SINSATIONS

WHAT COWARDS
FEATURING JOSEPH ADOMAVICIA

Society can try and label me. It can try to hold me back, crack jokes and tell me what I lack. And if I spend all my time listening to other people's opinions more than my own intuition, I'd be blind to all I'm missing. I'd be the composer of my own swan song walking a cavern of echoes alongside my enemies. People will always be greedy and are fine with being your frenemy. To them, it's more of a convenience to be the reason of your grievance; the earthquake causing the upheaval of someone else's character. Why discard deceit when you can be the manufacturer of the revival of someone's greatest insecurities? What cowards are the greedy? Who are so needy that they take what makes me so unique critique it for empty satisfaction?

-Joseph Adomavicia

But how come we can't choose who or what we say goodbye to first?

Like certain friendships and relationships

I know we have the opportunity to learn from one another

However, some of these situations, I'm like why do I even bother?

Never should a person make someone cry or evoke emotions so strong

I know everything that happens in your life does for a reason

Some of the reasons are becoming the same meaning I'm being repetitive

Some people are greedy, some with ill-intent and some don't know

For those that do, what cowards you are to sit up and consider yourself a friend

-Reggie Johnson

KAMIKAZE

You wanted the control
You took the captain's seat and wanted me to co-pilot this plane
That you didn't know was going to takeoff on a path off destruction
So much certainty amongst uncertainty
But the thought of having it all figured out
From the beginning plagued you
And I was that became of sick of it
And you hit the eject button
Launched yourself out of here as quick you led it
And I'm left here, on a kamikaze flight to nowhere
And if I just would've switched earlier
We could've avoided this crash

INCAPABLE

You treat affection like it's insatiable
So from the start, I wasn't capable
In the end, I wish it was a fable
What was the real deal?
You wanted everything in the world, but around me my lips are sealed
So quick to rebound
You wanted to be the center of attention
No offense to my defense, I had to remove you from mentions

CHASING LOVE

Keep chasing love
Instead of letting it chase you
You think having bodies under your belt will lead you to the right one
This isn't like racking up a killstreak, this isn't the same outcome
You might be MVP, but in the call of duty, you only chasing zombies
Mindless creatures we are and I'm not trying to let that haunt me
I've chased love once

SLOTH

One's ability to not care about one's self and their potential to better themselves

I'M DONE

I have no energy
No strength to fight with you
You've exhausted all of your resources
I have nothing left to give

REGGIE JOHNSON

NOT TODAY

I don't feel like it
Not today...
I'm not giving you energy
You've charged up so much built up aggression
That a simple Ki blast from you won't make me use an ounce
Of strength if you know what I'm Saiyan
I'll just lay here until you relax
And you'll either come and lay right beside me and say I'm sorry
Or come over to slap me, grab your clothes and leave

SINSATIONS

WINNERS & LOSERS

Sometimes it's better to take things slow

There isn't a story in the world that has the tortoise losing to the hare

But you...

You wanted to hop from one stage of this situationship

To the next stage, a relationship

To the next stage, a companionship

To the next stage, a unionship

When we miss the important one of all

All these ships you got docked, but you couldn't find a space for us

To be friends first

Everything moved so fast and I just wanted to take time

Develop what we had

But you wanted to win so bad

At your own game and in the end, you won

You won being yourself

And I learned a valuable lesson

Enjoy your trophy

LAZY
FEATURING RANDY MASCORRO

I don't want
To leave this bed
This tomb for my soul
This vacation from
The world
If darkness is a friend
I have all I need
And if sunshine
Goes away
I have already
Found a place
Solitude is
A smile
I don't want
To leave
This bed

-*Randy Mascorro*

I don't want
To leave this bed
This haven
This safe place
This place that makes you feel
At ease
Or reminds you of the pain
One minute, you can go
From happy to depressed
The next
My body doesn't have the
Strength to get up and leave
For a long time
It knows to return
The keeper of all your secrets
I don't want
To leave
This bed

-*Reggie Johnson*

FEEL

I don't want to feel like this

As I stay looking through my covers trying to reminisce

About that, about this

The decisions that led up to left me lifeless

Getting up is the motivation and I hadn't planned on it

I hadn't planned on the minutes, hours, days that I spent in this bed

Counting tears of the bullshit

All of the crying for nothing

And you just left me there

The note you left on my nightstand

"I'm sorry" is all it said

Never do I want to leave from this bed

HAUNTED

Feels like I'm not rushing to be in a relationship
While everyone's running laps
Maybe if I thought it was a relay
I could've had my life on track
Instead of worrying about jumping these hurdles of heartbreak
And heartache
Oh wells and it is what it is
To maybe meaningless sex to maybe even a couple kids
I'm taking each minute, second and hour one moment in a time
While everyone else out making moments to last a lifetime
Well in my lifetime, I want the time of my life
Not just the time is in the essence or the time is just right
I want this feeling everyday and I want to make it last all night
Make me last all night and I'll make it last forever
And I'll continue to wait for love and I'll wait forever

WRATH

REGGIE JOHNSON

Uncontrollable feelings of hatred and anger towards a person in a wish to seek revenge

SINSATIONS

RED
FEATURING J.R.

Regrettably, I've been here many a time, staring down a loaded gun done by my own doing- it always gets the best of me. I can't explain the seething rage that erupts from my pores and spleens with total detriment: it's like staring at the sun with both eyelids closed, only my mind is in a tumult of emotions clattering to be unfettered; red.

-J.R.

It's like you go numb...Everything starts tingling. Mind goes blank. All you see is white...when other see the red in my eyes. Don't need a cape to see the amount of bullshit I put up with...and I'm just sweeping my hoofs of steam hoping that something doesn't snap to make me lash out.

-Reggie Johnson

THE DAY THAT'LL LIVE IN INFAMY

Take me to that day...
That day that will live in infamy
Because the war we started rocked both our worlds
Not Kratos himself could help...
I became Atreus...
Someone stricken by your disappointment over and over
At first, I wanted acceptance
Your forgiveness
But then, it became anger
And I didn't care anymore
I really didn't...
Since you didn't...
You lashed out with your chains
And I continue to shoot an arrow through any type of friendship
All because I'm angry.

SINSATIONS

RED FLAMES & HURRICANES
FEATURING J.R.

Fractured knuckles and a bruised ego in exchange for a refined disposition, gentle men and words held no bearing in my part of town; and I've yet to find a way to say I'm in pain, without hurting myself even more in the process. I'm often reminded of what a fucking disaster I am, when left to sift through the pieces of my catastrophes. I bleed and weep and bleed and weep while pushing through with a blank face, "men face their problems in silence" is what my father said to me, but why do hurricanes howl when it's too late?

-J.R.

Not good enough
That feeling revs you up to the point that you're on a path to mental destruction
Literally see red because you couldn't see me
I guess it wasn't that black and white
That feeling...
Consoling is all need to douse the flames I've created because of my reactions
And when you put out some fires
It seems like all that ends up happening is letting off steam

-Reggie Johnson

REGGIE JOHNSON

AGAIN

Seeing you again right now
Is like waving a red cape in front of my face
For having to deal with this bullshit again
Go ándale somewhere
ya que encontraste una distracción en otra parte
así que corte mis cuernos de toro y déjame estar

THE TIME
FEATURING HALFOFYOU

The time it took to drain me out, was quicker than you thought. The time you ripped me apart was more vicious than the shark The times I was wholesome, you did me in
Just to leave your mark
The time I broke, I fixed me up
I dreamt of Noah's Ark
Apocalypse and heavy rains, my heart was turned about. The time.

-HalfOfYou

The time it took for you to come with this poor excuse of a friendship, a brotherhood. All the time in the world, but never would I thought that one of my own could stab me in the back. Might as well stabbed me from the front so I can look you in the eye when it happened. The time you betrayed one of the few people that had your back. Now I hold nothing, not even your bones. And I'll look you in the face and tell you this is the last time you'll ever do this to me again.

-Reggie Johnson

REGGIE JOHNSON

INNER TURMOIL
FEATURING J.R.

I've met aggression with aggression my whole life, that's the way I've dealt with emotion, but over the years I've slowly come to learn fire versus fire just makes for an inferno no one should ever have to feel. A lifetime spent cursing dark clouds is a lifetime not knowing the gift of rain. I've been under so much pressure lately—like a star at the end of its cycle, but I don't know whether I'm exploding or imploding.

-J.R.

I've played this game for so long. The pent up anger is just my heart being engulfed in flames as my body catches the wildfire. Yielding not a single ounce of growth to happen from this young stature. One cannot create new life from decrepit soil. But I continue to plant that seed in my mind hoping one day, I will change the outcome.

-Reggie Johnson

SINSATIONS

EMOTIONAL WRECK
FEATURING J.R.

Many times my own emotions have melted those around me to their core. Try as I may to turn passion into fire, it seems directed false may have the wrong intent. And yet I'm reminded of my fire—you don't have to burn yourself or those you love to be the light in someone's life.

-J.R.

Heartbreak in the past. Seeing red went from being thorns from roses to thorns from my bleeding heart oozing out of my pores. The art of surprise. Silent, but deadly. Instant kill as if you were in the call of duty. I guess I didn't have a UAV. Couldn't believe all you did was hurt me and everything that I said that resulted from it is like you deserved it. The lashing out, the arguments—it was just yelling. A lot of it and then silence. No one wins ever, but love will prevail.

-Reggie Johnson

REGGIE JOHNSON

ENVY

SINSATIONS

The thought of being discontent or uncomfortable of another based on one's success, possessions or luck

REGGIE JOHNSON

JEKYLL & HYDE

I've experienced envy on all different levels
It always surprises me
How can one be so jealous of me and vice versa
It happens though...
It's a feeling that just takes over
Look at Mr. Hyde hiding
We all can't be Jekyll for too long

SINSATIONS

STRICKEN
FEATURING B.A. HUNTER

Why don't I deserve the peaceful bliss of death's breathless kiss? Could it be that I have tried to die, so many times, but was only met with unanswered cries to the sky? Just, please, cut the chains, let me keep the pain, and leave me for the sun to be slain, drink in its flames. What must I do, to trade places with you? My heart and lungs even staged a coup, my soul is turning beginning to turn blue. Suffocating on a fightless acceptance with the black veil because I never dare ever again exhale. Come back already. They need you. Not me. It should've taken me.

-*B.A. Hunter*

It's like a sickness and it's like I'm plagued by it so much. Everything can be going fine and the next minute, I become green. Queasy from certain situations, cause and effects, moments that got me to a point where you become no longer tolerable for the time being and once stricken, it gets worse before it gets better. And it happens every time, but it gets better, because I need it to. I cannot stay like this forever.

-*Reggie Johnson*

REGGIE JOHNSON

WASTE
FEATURING B.A. HUNTER

I have always longed for my words to be read by the world. Admired not through fancy gimmicks, but by an equal appreciation of life. Yet of course, the pages desecrated by others with ink penned by lies collect dust on shelves around the market. Such a waste. It should be me. My typewriter now wishes it was their laptop. A shame how talent is replaced by greed.

-B.A. Hunter

Sometimes I sit and think about... this piece didn't get enough likes, I don't have enough followers. My psyche succumbs to the false realities that I have to rely on millennial validations in order to feel good about myself. And somehow, I'm depreciating myself not giving my best work. I feel like such a waste. I wish that I had their amount of followers. Ashamed that I feel I can stoop down to the level of caring about miscellaneous things out of my control.

-Reggie Johnson

SINSATIONS

SIGNS
FEATURING B.A. HUNTER

If I had his gold in my pocket, her smiles would last longer than the miles we would travel from corner to corner of the world. His love is traded with dirty paper, but mine is painted carefully on signs that only she can read. I don't feel worthy enough to be in her light, in his shadow, sharing to death.

-B.A. Hunter

Keep friends close, enemies closer. People you can't trust the closest The amount of rope you give a person determines the actions that result from it. Too short of a rope, you become too involved. Too long of a rope, you began to miss them. Give them their own rope and they'll lasso someone else in and it's your personal woes that make they can just come in and takeover everything you worked so hard for. So easily and to think we are just gonna let it happen.

-Reggie Johnson

REGGIE JOHNSON

ANIMAL FARM
FEATURING HALFOFYOU

Naïve and candid did the Little Calf play within the boundaries of the pasture. Along came another and began to graze, the beginning of the ugly. Little Calf took to anger in a twisted, cruel way and began to plot. Unheard of to dine with him, he took to the brain, a sick feeling of anger and callousness, disregarding for the calf took to starving of the pasture for them both. Now either could eat, as both simmered down, with a shrug and frown. Little Calf fell into eternal slumber.

-HalfOfYou

In a world full of sheep and cattle, we all aim to not live in an Animal Farm view of the world. Everyone aiming to break out from the herd. When we see someone that does, at first we feel happiness that we too can get out. Then, something comes over us as we realize, how the hell did they get out and why haven't I? We become bitter and our actions become bolder. To the point that we are trapped inside our own Animal Farm mentally.

-Reggie Johnson

SINSATIONS

GREEN
FEATURING B.A. HUNTER

How sweet it must be to taste the light of death, become a lover with darkness, an end to this pain called life? To be missed by many, remembered by enemies, to be forever held by the beautifully cold earth. Left to only dream in peaceful sleep. Oh, my deer grim reaper, please, come take me to your keep.

-B.A. Hunter

Green should only be the color of money and plants as we should be enriched by either the power of the dollar or the power of life. Green should never hidden inside us that all of a sudden, we become our own stylized incredible hulks that not a single character from Marvel could defeat. Marvel at that. The fact that we could possess so much jealously towards something, someone and somehow the things that we dislike in them, we find a common interest if we just take the time to understand the situation.

-Reggie Johnson

ALL YOU EVER DO
FEATURING B.A. HUNTER

All you ever do is sit and whine about stupid shit, wasting time. Safety behind a screen unaware of how unfair life truly is, but aware you tear down dreams.
Imagine the gold I would have been able to forge words carved from diamonds. If I had your silver spoon, instead of a cardboard roof, starving while tears fall onto my crayon-drawn passport to the moon, which fuller proves money is not everything.
You cannot buy it all, some things you have to be born with.

-B.A. Hunter

All you ever do is bark orders like it's your way or no way. Sometimes a screen can only be a place to get out of everything you want to say. Because there is no point of face-to-face. I only dream to end my nightmares and to finally wake up from the bullshit I was put through. Money really is not enough. I cannot buy realness for an inanimate object pretending to have feelings. Some things I guess you don't have to be born with.

-Reggie Johnson

SINSATIONS

WHAT HAPPENED TO YOU?
FEATURING B.A. HUNTER

Look at yourself. Everything that you ever wanted in the palm of your hands. I somehow, let it all slip through mine. She even looks at you with a great smile, unlike the darkness I'm forgotten lost in, not even leaving behind a frown. The past full of memories choking me with claws and at this point, I do not fight back. Letting air escape, the tightening around my throat and letting the void wash over my eyes. And you...will live on, holding the heart of the world in your chest. But I bet you won't ever wonder what happened to you.

-B.A. Hunter

Eyes bled green as the hulk within began bleeding rage seeing her with another. And just like that, Bruce Banner wouldn't appear again. ¿Qué tenía él que yo no tenía? ¿Qué hizo él que no pude hacer? As strong as I were for us, your heart was strong for him. So go be with him. Be fine with knowing you ran off with someone's heart and never left them the same.

-Reggie Johnson

REGGIE JOHNSON

THE LIGHT
FEATURING B.A. HUNTER

It is not fair that you get bathe in all the light undeserved, as I starve in this endless darkness iniquitously. What gave you the right to down out my voice? Who gave you this entitled title to step on all of us? How could one be so blind with so many eyes everywhere? Where did your beating heart go? I want the power you wield, hand in hand, so I may cleanse myself of all the sins you say I have.

-*B.A. Hunter*

I bask in the light because you envelope darkness so easily that it's stamped on your forehead and when I send for it, you deliver right on time. It's annoying. I thought my actions would be enough, but you left me to keep reiterating things like a broken record playing that annoying one hit wonder that you've loved to hate. I wish I could trade places with you one day. To not have the burden of having to control each and everything and just become as mindless and detached as you are.

-*Reggie Johnson*

PRIDE

REGGIE JOHNSON

A corrupt sense of one's personal views or one's values

VALUE

One cannot equate my value to monetary
means
I'm priceless, but I'm worth it all
Incomparable...
You have not and will not ever
Some people try to and I hate it every time
This is my ultimate sin
I love to indulge that I can't get enough
And I could care less if you have had enough

REGGIE JOHNSON

I
FEATURING ROBERT VENEGAS

Can you justify a tempered lie based on a wish that they told you hope for when you look into the midnight sky? Pay for truths in rubies and stack bills for they told you to get, and what to want, and what to strive for. I'll strive for greatness like LeBron in the post, 30 million dollar dreams for my self beliefs. I love me some me, and can't be satisfied with following the dreams of he.

-Robert Venegas

I strive to be the best. To be skillful in all that I partake and to me I get a rush off of it. The endorphins rush through me flooding my occipitals until I can't see that this very thing that helps me rise up makes the commodity that is pressure arise as well. Putting it all on me. Afraid to fail. I do this constantly and it's worse when you point it out.

-Reggie Johnson

TOLL

It takes a toll on me...
I pay for it more and more
When all it asks for is change
Change you want to give by penny, nickel
and dime'n me
Not at my expense
Not worth the pursuit of my happiness
Not worth any cost

REGGIE JOHNSON

SELF
FEATURING ROBERT VENEGAS

In the office of my therapist, I see where I've been and what I've done. Accomplishments that build like bricks to the pyramids, but what is there left to feed the taste of climbing mounds of impossible? I've yet to climb Olympus and live amongst the gods. Like Hercules before me, my feet shall grace the silent halls of existence. Tomorrow is yet to come, but years have passed since I've disappointed the mirror self.

-*Robert Venegas*

I've should've lost myself. Like I got lost in my ways. It was all over a few months which felt like a couple days. Seven is all it took, but you already had me weak. Te quitaste mis palabras when I couldn't even speak I was frozen. Open like a Disney movie, but all you said was to let it go. You sung it over and over until you made it a hit single. And now I have these lyrics. And I'm wasting them thinking about you. Llorando sobre lágrimas secas and now this supposed to be about you. Pride won't let my heart lose and I continue to play these games. Losing myself, one should do the same.

-*Reggie Johnson*

SINSATIONS

I FEEL

No one can take away my pride
But I feel like a bunch of people lying around me
Got comfortable, they lying on me
They take me kindness for naivety
Be the parade on my rainy day
But I won't let that happen
Whether or not you stand by me

I, (PART II)
FEATURING ROBERT VENEGAS

I am bound by others blindness. Their bluntness is obscene. I am on a caravan through tortured lands and all their eyes rely on those who claim mad. Confused are they who haven't reached this pinnacle of Godly Kings. I will not be moved by seasonal ends. For I am the center that the world shows bend.

-Robert Venegas

Sometimes I have to push myself. Sometimes I get caught up in my own self. I get comfortable in my ways that I feel like everyone else should just respect them and I don't want to leave the comfort. I don't want to leave the console or the security. I'm not ready for the change.

-Reggie Johnson

THE COLLECTIVE

A SPECIAL THANKS TO EVERYONE INVOLVED ON THIS PROJECT
FOLLOW ALL OF THE WRITERS ON INSTAGRAM

MITCH GREEN: @MITCH_GRN
ASHLEY LUCAS: @A.R.LUCAS
JOSEPH ADOMAVICIA: @J.ADOMAVICIA
RANDY MASCORRO: @RANDYMASCORRO
J.R.: @_THE_WOLFS_HOWL
B.A. HUNTER: @B.A.HUNTER
ROBERT VENEGAS: @ROBERTJVENEGAS
HALFOFYOU: @HALFOFYOU

BECAUSE THE INK NEVER DRIES UP
FOLLOW ME ON MY SOCIAL MEDIA

FACEBOOK: @R.D.JOHNSON
TWITTER: @R_D_JOHNSON
INSTAGRAM: @R.D.JOHNSON

www.ingramcontent.com/pod-product-compliance
Lightning Source LLC
Chambersburg PA
CBHW032050290426
44110CB00012B/1031